The New
Brown Bag

The Singing Bowl

The New
Brown Bag

The Singing Bowl
26 Children's Sermons
with Activities

Randy Hammer

THE
PILGRIM
PRESS
Cleveland

For Luke and Josiah, with much love and affection,
and also to the children of the United Church, Chapel on the Hill,
of Oak Ridge, Tennessee.

The Pilgrim Press, 700 Prospect Avenue, Cleveland, Ohio 44115, thepilgrimpress.com
© 2009 Randy Hammer

GNT designates Scripture taken from the Good News Translation, second edition,
copyright © 1992 by American Bible Society. Used by permission. NRSV designates
the New Revised Standard Version Bible, copyright © 1989 by the Division of
Christian Education of the National Council of the Churches of Christ in the U.S.A.
Used by permission.

Printed in the United States of America on acid-free paper

13 12 11 10 09   5 4 3 2 1

Library of Congress Cataloging-in-Publication Data

Hammer, Randy, 1955-
    The singing bowl : 26 children sermons with activities / Randy Hammer.
        p. cm.
    ISBN 978-0-8298-1851-2 (alk. paper)
    1. Children's sermons. 2. Sermons, American--21st century. I. Title.
BV4315.H2787 2009
252'.53--dc22
                                    2009002974

Contents

Preface

This book is a companion book to my previous book, *The Talking Stick: 40 Children's Sermons with Activities*, published by The Pilgrim Press in 2007, although the books can also be used independently. Many of the stories and lessons to be found in this small volume have been developed and shared with children of all ages at First Congregational Church, United Church of Christ, of Albany, New York, and the United Church of Oak Ridge, Tennessee. There are stories and lessons that may be used for special Sundays in the year, such as Reign of Christ Sunday, the Sunday near Thanksgiving, Sundays during Advent and Epiphany, the Sunday near Martin Luther King Jr.'s birthday, and on days when Holy Communion or baptism will be celebrated or when there will be an emphasis on stewardship or missions. Generally speaking, my preference in using scripture passages with children is the Good News Translation, designated by GNT, because it is often considered particularly suitable for children. However, occasionally a different translation is preferred, most often the New Revised Standard Version. For each scriptural basis of the stories included the suggested translation is noted. I am happy to share these stories with all those who have a love of children and a love of bringing children and stories together for the enjoyment and betterment of all.

Introduction

Where Does the Inspiration for Children's Sermons Come From?

Sometimes people ask me how I come up with ideas for the children's sermons I write. As you might imagine, ideas come from a variety of sources. One primary requisite is a keen sense of observation of the world around you. For instance, the other day I was stopped in traffic behind a truck that had a long padlock dangling from the back door clasp. The padlock was unlocked and very easily could have bounced out of its hole and onto the roadway. And I thought to myself, *What would I do were I to find such a nice padlock on the roadway?* Since childhood I have been fascinated with padlocks for some reason, way back to my younger days when my grandmother gave my cousin and me one of those tiny toy padlocks that could be purchased at dime stores. It was a great delight for me to put that tiny padlock on the small treasure chest where I placed my most prized boyhood treasures. But I digress. Were I to find an expensive padlock on the roadway, no matter how nice a lock it was, it would be no good apart from the key to go with it. A lock and a key go together. They need each other.

How much like people, I thought to myself. So the idea for a future children's sermon was born. Such children's sermons seeds are abundant in our everyday lives, if we have eyes to see them. A brass bowl, salt, spilled milk, a piece of rough wood, pottery, a bottle of perfume, and a bag of pennies are some of the everyday objects that inspired children's sermons in this volume.

Another source of inspiration for children's sermons, as I have noted in previous collections, is the world of nature. There is no greater teacher than the natural world around us. A coconut, birds, pebbles, and a mother hen have much to teach us, if we have time to learn.

People can provide an excellent source of inspiration for children's sermons. Harold Wilkie, a strong voice and advocate for people with disabilities; Clara Barton, who organized the American Red Cross; and of course, Jesus of Nazareth—history is rich with persons who inspire us to be all that we can be.

And what about places? The seaside, a dark forest, a carpenter's workshop, a village in a developing country, and a dam are places that cry out for a story.

Finally, ancient tales that can be given new life provide an unlimited resource and well of inspiration that can never run dry. In addition to Bible stories, Aesop's Fables and historical legends, such as the one about the Pilgrims and the five kernels of corn, are rich reservoirs of material.

So, as with my previous books of children's sermons, may this small volume serve as a springboard for your own imagination as you develop a keen observation of life, nature, people, places, and great literature of the ages.

1
The Singing Bowl
All Things Can
Give Praise to God

Scripture: Psalm 150 GNT

Object for Sharing: A bronze singing bowl and baton that can be purchased at such stores as Ten Thousand Villages.

Presentation: Choose a Sunday when special music or a variety of musical instruments will be used in worship.

Have you ever known a bowl that could sing? Well, there are some bowls that can do just that. Listen closely and you will hear this bowl sing (*run baton around the rim of the bronze bowl to create a "song"*). Did you hear it?

Monks sometimes use this type of bowl to call people to worship, prayer, or meditation. Not only does it sing when rubbed the right way, it also gives off a wonderful chime (*strike the bowl with the baton while holding the bowl on the outstretched palm of your hand*). Isn't that nice?

In the Hebrew book of Psalms we hear the psalmist calling upon all things to sing praise to God. Listen to what the psalmist says and see if you can pick out an unusual instrument or object that he calls upon to sing praise to God (*read Psalm 150*).

"Praise God with trumpet sound;
Praise God with lute and harp!

Praise God with strings and pipe!
Praise God with clanging cymbals;
Praise God with loud clashing cymbals!
Praise God with singing bowls!"
(Actually, I added that last line. But I think the psalmist would agree, don't you? Then the psalmist sums it all by saying:)
"Let everything that breathes praise the Lord!"

I think that the writer of this psalm was trying to say that everything on earth—living creatures and nonliving things alike—has been created to sing praise to God.

FOLLOW-UP: Conclude with the children returning to their seats as all sing the first stanza of "All Creatures of Our God and King."

2

A Hard Shell
or a Soft Shell?
We Will Get Along Better in Life
If We Are Somewhat Flexible

SCRIPTURE: Matthew 5:23–24, 44–45 GNT

OBJECTS FOR SHARING: A coconut and a sponge Nerf ball.

PRESENTATION: Punch a hole in the coconut and drain the milk beforehand.

Have you ever known someone who was inflexible? Can someone tell us what inflexible means? Someone who is inflexible might be described as hardheaded. Hardheaded folk must always be right. Whenever there is a disagreement, they never give in. And if someone does something to upset them, they never forgive. They are inflexible. They won't bend or give in. (*Raise hammer, making it appear that you are going to strike the coconut, but then stop as though you have changed your mind. Do so in such a way so as to build suspense.*)

Yet other folk are flexible. They are sometimes willing to admit that they are wrong and others are right. Whenever there is a disagreement, they are willing to reconsider and sometimes give in. If someone else does something to upset them, they are willing to forgive. Flexible. Willing to bend or give in. (*Strike Nerf sponge ball with hammer so that children can see it bounce back.*)

Sometimes it is okay to be inflexible and stand our ground, especially when we feel we are standing up for what is right, for example, standing up for another child who's being bullied. At other times, it is better to be flexible and give in and forgive, so as to make for peace. As followers of Jesus, we are called to "do justice"—to do the right thing—but also to be peacemakers and forgive others as we want to be forgiven.

The trouble is when we are always one or the other. If we are always flexible and willing to give in—for example, always letting the big bully get his way—what might happen? Right—people might soon walk all over us and take advantage of us in any way they can. But if we were always inflexible and unwilling to give in—for example, always standing up to the bully, no matter what—what might happen to us? Right—if sometime something were to happen when we didn't get our way, it might devastate us. It might crush us. (*Strike coconut with the hammer so that it shatters.*)

Those who know when to be flexible tend to get along much better in life than those who are always inflexible.

FOLLOW-UP: After making sure none of the children is allergic to nuts, share the coconut meat and explore together God's gift of coconuts, how they grow, what other lessons they teach us, etc.

3
Who Is This Man?
Jesus Changes Lives

SCRIPTURE: Matthew 14:22–27, 32–33 GNT

OBJECT FOR SHARING: A picture of a small boat on the Sea of Galilee.

PRESENTATION: A fishing net, some fishing buckets, a rain slicker like fishermen wear, and other similar props will reinforce the story.

Have you ever wondered what anyone standing on the lakeshore might have thought that early morning when Jesus came walking toward the disciples on the water? What if there had been a fisherman there on the shore, coming in from a night of fishing? What do you think he might have been thinking? Perhaps he would have told his story something like this:

"I've been out on the lake all night fishing. I haven't caught much, but enough to make it worth my time. The waves start getting rougher, so I know a storm is coming. I think it best that I row to shore and clean my nets and get on home before the storm comes.

"I've just stepped out of my boat, in about knee-deep water, and am trying to pull it up on to the shore when I see this man walking down the shore toward the water. The sun is beginning to come up in the east, so there isn't very much light yet. And the dark clouds rolling in make it darker than it would usually be that time of morning. The point I am getting at is it is just light enough for me to make out the figure of a man walking down the shore, but not light enough to make out who he is.

"I stop cleaning my net long enough to watch that man because something doesn't seem right. He just keeps walking out into the water, right into those rough waves that are crashing in on the shore. But as he walks into the water, the water doesn't rise up around him. It's as though he's walking right on top of the water! I can see the bottom edge of his robe dragging across the surface of the water. I must have stayed out on the lake way too long, I think to myself, because my eyes are playing tricks on me!

"I stand there on the shore leaning against the side of my boat as I watch that man walk right out into the middle of the lake to a little boat full of men who are being tossed about by the waves. The men are frightened, I can tell. They're yelling to the man, 'Save us! Please, Master, save us!'

"One of the men actually climbs over the edge of the boat and tries to walk toward the one walking on the water. But in no time he starts to sink, and the man walking on the water reaches out his hand and pulls him to safety. Both of them climb into the boat with the others, and immediately the winds die down and the waves become calm.

"I can't believe what I've witnessed. *Who is this man?* I say to myself, that even the wind and the waves obey him? I can tell by the way they bow before him that the men in the boat worship the one who's just saved them. I feel a change in myself as well. Truly this man must be the Son of God, I decide. Though no one else sees me do it, I too bow down toward the man who's been walking on water. How can one meet such an extraordinary man and not honor him?"

FOLLOW-UP: Ask the children if they have ever been in a boat in the midst of a storm and what they did. Or what they would do or how they would feel if, like the disciples, they found themselves in a similar situation.

4
Through the Dark Forest[1]
A True Friend Stands By in Times of Trouble

SCRIPTURES: Proverbs 17:17, 18:24 GNT

OBJECT FOR SHARING: A picture of a dark forest. Better yet, a picture of Dorothy of *The Wizard of Oz* walking through the dark forest.

PRESENTATION: If possible, darken the worship space when sharing this story to enhance the visual effects.

Have you ever been in a dark, dark forest? Well, do you remember that scene in *The Wizard of Oz* where Dorothy is walking through the dark, dark forest and singing "Lions, and tigers, and bears, oh my!"? Can you say that with me? "Lions, and tigers, and bears, oh my!"

There is an old story about two friends who were traveling together through a dark, dark forest. Suddenly a big, black bear appeared. One of the two friends hurried and climbed up a tree and remained hidden among the branches.

The other friend, who was unable to climb, knew he would be

caught by the bear any second. So he fell down on the ground and pretended to be dead. Now, the man had heard that a bear will not touch someone who is dead. So when the bear came up to smell him, near his ear, the man held his breath and remained as still as he could be. The bear, thinking the man to be dead, walked away.

After the bear had gone, the man who had climbed the tree asked the one who had played dead what the bear had whispered in his ear. "The bear told me," the man who had played dead replied, "to never again travel through the dark forest with a friend who runs away when trouble comes."

The scripture says that friends always show their love, and there is a friend who is closer than a brother or sister. In other words, a true friend is one who will walk with us through the dark times and not run away. Try and think of a time when you were such a true friend to someone that you didn't abandon him or her during a hard time.

FOLLOW-UP: Show and discuss a video clip from *The Wizard of Oz* where Dorothy and her friends are walking through the dark forest.

1. Adapted from *Aesop's Fables.*

5
Salt Locked in a Box
Like Salt, We Are Meant to Be Free to Flavor Our World

Scripture: Matthew 5:13–14 NRSV

Objects for Sharing: A small, lockable treasure chest that can be found at craft supply stores. Place some salt inside the chest and then place a lock on it prior to beginning the story.

Presentation: Why not consider presenting this story on a day when there will be a potluck luncheon or picnic?

You see that I have brought a small treasure chest with me today. Treasure chests have been used for hundreds of years to store all kinds of things. If you had a treasure chest, what do you think you would store in it? (*Give time for answers.*) Very interesting.

Well, I decided to pour all our salt into this chest and keep it locked up tight. That way it will be safe. And I don't have to worry about anyone stealing my salt. I'll never open it, and I'll never see it, and I'll never touch it. Does that sound like a pretty good idea? No? Why not?

You are exactly right. Salt is not intended to be locked up in a treasure chest, never to be seen again. No, salt is meant to be used for such things as flavoring food and to make it taste better. Many people use salt to preserve food for the future. The early American settlers used salt to preserve dried fish and other things. And has anyone ever eaten country ham? Salt is used to cure and preserve ham as well. Salt can also be used to heal infections in the body. When we have a sore throat, gargling with warm salt water can make it feel better and heal faster.

Yes, salt is just one of the many good gifts that God gave us to use. If we lock up salt in a treasure chest and throw away the key, it will do no one any good.

In the same way, we are to share ourselves with the world. Each of us has a witness, a gift, a word of good news to share with others. Each of us is called to make the world a more beautiful, more pleasant, more flavorful place. But often we are tempted to lock away our witness and gifts and words of good news and not share them with the world. But that is not why God gave us the gifts that we have. The good gifts that we have been given are meant to be unlocked (*unlock the treasure chest and open the lid*) and shared so as to make the lives of others better.

FOLLOW-UP: Explore with the children the many uses of salt and how salt was such a prized commodity in the time of Jesus.

6

Birds Don't Have Hands
Persons with Disabilities Are Beautiful People

Scripture: John 9:1–3 GNT

Object for Sharing: A picture of your favorite bird

Presentation: This story will work well on the Sunday when the congregation is thinking about justice for those who live with disabilities.

Do you like birds? I like birds, too. Indeed, birds are some of the most beautiful creatures created by God. What is your favorite bird? My favorite bird is the cardinal (*or whatever bird might be your particular favorite*).

I suppose you've noticed that birds don't have hands. They have what we might call arms, their wings that they use to fly and bathe themselves. But birds don't have hands to pick up things like you and I do. So to pick up something they have to use their beaks, or mouths, or their claws, or feet. But the fact that birds don't have hands doesn't make them any less beautiful, does it? In fact, birds might look funny if they did have hands.

You know, there are a few people in the world who do not have hands either. Perhaps something didn't quite work out right when they were developing before they were born. Or perhaps they were involved in an accident that caused them to lose their hands, perhaps their arms, too. In Jesus' day many people thought that any type of disability was punishment from God for some wrong that had been done. But Jesus knew, and today we know, that this is not the case.

There was a man, a very special man, named Harold Wilkie. Harold was born with no arms. So to do everyday things like you and I do that we don't even think about—like pick up a spoon to eat our morning cereal, or brush our teeth, or put on our sweater—Harold had to learn to use his mouth or his feet.

But Harold didn't let his disability stop him. He became a minister in the United Church of Christ and excelled at many things. Harold, as you might imagine, spoke up for persons with disabilities.

Many people, I am sure, when they looked at Harold thought he looked funny or different. The fact that he didn't have any arms probably made some people feel uncomfortable. But it is not arms or hands that make people beautiful. It is everything else about their life that makes them beautiful.

Just as birds that don't have any hands are beautiful, persons with disabilities are beautiful, too. We can see that if we look beyond what people don't have and then recognize the individual beauty that God gave them to share with the world.

FOLLOW-UP: Invite the children to share memories of when they encountered someone who was different and how they felt. Seek to dispel some of the myths and negative feelings that surround those who have disabilities of various sorts.

7

Spilled Milk Can't Be Gathered Back Up
Words We Speak Cannot Be Retrieved

Scriptures: Proverbs 12:18, 18:20–21 GNT

Objects for Sharing: A big bowl or pan of dry sand and a clear glass filled with milk.

Presentation: This story will work well when the topic of the day is inclusivity.

Can you help me with a scientific experiment? For our experiment, I have brought a big bowl of sand and a glass of milk. Here is what we are going to do. I am going to pour this glass of milk all around this bowl of dry sand (*pour glass of milk all around the top of the sand*). Now, let's let it soak in for a moment.

Now for the experiment. I would like for you to help me gather the milk—just the milk, no sand—back up again and put it back in the glass. How might we do that?

Well, I believe you are correct. There is no way to gather the milk back up again and put it back in the glass the way that it was before.

No way, never, no how. So I guess the old saying, "There is no need to cry over spilled milk," is true after all.

But there is an even greater lesson for us in this experiment that has nothing to do with spilled milk and a whole lot to do with spilled words. Just as we are in danger of tipping over a glass of milk and spilling it all over the floor, we also are in danger of spilling words that cannot be gathered back up again. When we thoughtlessly say hurtful words to others—words like "I don't like you," or "You're ugly," or "You're too fat," or "You're too skinny," and so on—we have spilled those words out into the world and they can never be gathered back up again. Once such hurtful words are gone, they can't be taken back.

As the wise book of Proverbs reminds us, each of us is responsible for the words we utter. And if we say words that get us into trouble, then we will have to suffer the consequences. For instance, there are some words that we might think we're saying in a joking manner that could cause a lot of problems and get us into big trouble. Can you think of three little words that you would not want your friend to blurt out to you after you've disagreed about something? How about "I hate you"?

It pays us to think before we speak because our words can cause a lot of hurt. Like milk spilled in a bowl of sand, hurtful words spilled forth in anger cannot be gathered back again.

FOLLOW-UP: Ask the children to share something that someone said to them that was very hurtful. Often children thoughtlessly say hurtful things without realizing just how hurtful they are. As they share with one another, they should become more sensitive about the words they speak.

8
Good morning! And Welcome to Wal-Mart!
Everyone Likes to Be Welcomed

SCRIPTURE: Hebrews 13:2 NRSV

OBJECT FOR SHARING: Yellow smiley face stickers

PRESENTATION: If you really want to get creative, secure and don a blue "Wal-Mart" vest for the presentation.

Good morning! (*Shake hands with each child and greet each child alike. Also, give each child a smiley face sticker.*) And welcome to Wal-Mart. Good morning!

What's wrong with saying that? Well, you're right. This is *not* Wal-Mart. This is (*say the name of your church*). But there is also something right with saying "Good morning, and welcome," isn't there?

Wal-Mart learned that people like to be greeted and welcomed. And so whenever you go to a Wal-Mart store, there will always be someone there at the front door to greet you and to say, "Good morning" or "Good afternoon, and welcome to Wal-Mart."

So this morning I want to say to each of you, "Good morning, and welcome to (*say the name of your church*)!"

But I also want to ask for your help. There are going to be a lot of new people—new children included—who are going to walk through those front doors the next few months. And all of those new people will be hoping that someone says to them, "Good morning, welcome to (*say the name of your church*)!" I would like to ask each of you to help me welcome all the new children who come here this year by saying those few important words—"Good morning; welcome to (*say the name of your church*)!" Can you do that?

FOLLOW-UP: Explore with the children some of the other practical ways that they can make newcomers feel welcome.

9
Something Beautiful for God
God Likes to Make Us Beautiful

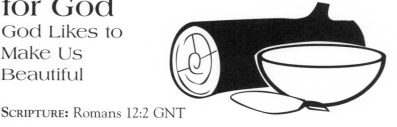

SCRIPTURE: Romans 12:2 GNT

OBJECTS FOR SHARING: A rough piece of wood, a carving tool, and a finished woodcraft from the same kind of stock.

PRESENTATION: This lesson will work well when prayer is the theme of the day.

Good morning! Have you ever seen anything like this before? (*Remove the rough piece of wood from the mystery bag.*) It's just an old, rough piece of wood that I brought from a woodshop. It's not very pretty, is it? And it doesn't look like it would be worth much, does it? And probably none of us would want it lying around on our coffee table at home, would we?

But a skilled hand can take an old, rough piece of wood like this and create something beautiful like this (*remove crafted and finished piece of wood for all to see*). By carving down the rough edges, and shaping it with a tool like this (*reveal carving tool*), and then sanding it and finishing it, you can create a beautiful wooden candleholder or bowl. But for that to happen the wood must give itself to be worked by the skilled craftsperson.

You know, it is sort of like that with people. Sometimes people can be pretty rough. We do things we shouldn't do. We live our lives in ways that are not very nice and that are hurtful to others. To be honest, sometimes people are not very appealing.

But God is like the skilled craftsperson who wants to take our lives and make something beautiful out of them. God wants to work away the rough spots in our lives like saying hurtful things to others, fighting, jealously, and so on. And God wants to sand us smooth and put a nice, loving finish on us. And one primary way that God does that is through prayer.

When we spend time in prayer every day asking God to make us into the persons God wants us to be, then just as with this old rough piece of wood that becomes something beautiful, so our lives become something beautiful, too.

FOLLOW-UP: Prior to the lesson, make a short video of a craftsperson creating a wood craft and show the video to the children.

10
Giving What We Have
God Is Happy When We Give What We Have to Give

SCRIPTURE: John 12:1–8 GNT

OBJECT FOR SHARING: A bottle of perfume for the children to smell (but be careful about spraying because of allergies).

PRESENTATION: This lesson will work well during stewardship season.

What do you know about perfume? Some perfumes smell very strong, don't they? Some are so strong they can be overpowering. Another thing about perfume is that it can be very expensive. Some perfumes sell for hundreds, perhaps even thousands of dollars a bottle. That is amazing, isn't it?

There is a story in the Bible about a woman who once poured an entire bottle of perfume on Jesus' feet. Why do you think she did that? Well, everyone in the house that day wondered too. They just couldn't understand it. And a lot of them started complaining, saying the perfume could have been sold and the money given to the poor.

But Jesus commended the woman. Because he knew that the woman, Mary, wanted to show her great love for him and she did so in the only way she knew how. She had a very expensive bottle of perfume that was used when people died. Back in those days, when a family member died, the other members washed the person's body and then put strong smelling perfumes and spices on the body before they buried it.

Perhaps the expensive bottle of perfume was the only thing Mary had to show her love for Jesus. And so that is what she did.

All of us have different gifts and different ways of showing our love for Jesus and for others. And when we give what we have to give, God is happy with that, just as Jesus was happy with Mary's gift of perfume.

FOLLOW-UP: Lead the children in making "perfume" by mixing sweet-smelling spices or flowers such as lilacs with water or olive oil.

11
Good for Nothing
We Can Be Good and
Serve Others for Nothing

Scripture: 1 Peter 4:10 NRSV

Object for Sharing: A "bill" written out as noted below.

Presentation: This story will work well during stewardship season.

One morning Benjamin came down to breakfast with a neatly folded piece of paper in his hand. Benjamin laid the piece of paper where his mother sat at the table. On the outside it said, "For Mother."

As Benjamin sat down to eat his breakfast, his mother opened the piece of paper. She couldn't believe what she saw. It was a bill! Can anyone tell us what a bill is? That is correct: a bill is something someone sends us, telling us that we owe money. This is what Benjamin's bill said:

<u>Mother owes Benjamin:</u>
For being good $.50
For running errands $.50

For taking music lessons	$.50
For taking out the trash	$.50
For everything else	$1.00
Total	$3.00

Benjamin's mother didn't say a word. But she folded the paper again and put it in her pocket.

When Benjamin came in for lunch, he was happy to see three one-dollar bills on his plate along with the note he had left at breakfast. But he was surprised to find another note underneath them both that said, "For Benjamin." Benjamin opened up his note and this is what he read:

Benjamin owes Mother:	
For being good to him	$0
For cooking his meals	$0
For making his bed	$0
For taking care of him when he was sick	$0
For everything else	$0
Total	$0

Benjamin got the message and felt bad. So he took the $3.00 and placed it in his mother's hands and said, "Here are the $3.00, Mother. Let me love you and be good for nothing."

You see, it's okay to sometimes want to earn some money. But sometimes we need to just be good and help out around the house because that is the right thing to do. The way of Jesus is to be "good for nothing"—that is, good for no cost at all

---

FOLLOW-UP: Brainstorm with the children the many ways that others serve them each day, as well as ways they can make a point to "be good for nothing."

12
Coffee Can Faith[2]
Gifts Are Not Intended to Be Hidden

SCRIPTURE: Ephesians 4:10–12 GNT

OBJECT FOR SHARING: A coffee can containing some coins.

PRESENTATION: This lesson is quite suitable for stewardship season.

How many of you have coffee cans full of money hidden in your back yard? Well, if you did, you wouldn't want to tell me, would you? However, years ago it was common for people to hide money in coffee cans in their lawns because they didn't trust the banks.

There is an old story about a man who buried some gold in a can in a field where he thought no one would find it. Every day the man would go to the place where the gold was buried and he would stand there and look down at the ground and gloat over his gold.

Well, one day a child in town followed the man and hid behind a tree and watched as he stood there talking to himself about the gold that was buried beneath his feet. When the man left, the child dug up the gold and ran away with it.

The next day when the man came to gloat over his can of gold, he found an empty hole in the ground. He had an angry fit. "My gold! My gold!" the man cried, jumping up and down. A traveler happened to be passing by that way and saw what was going on. "What's all the excitement about?" the traveler asked the man as he continued to jump up and down and yell. "I had my gold buried here in a can," the man explained, "and every day I would come here and think about it. Now it is gone. Someone took it."

"Well," the traveler said, "you shouldn't be so sad. Even when you had the gold it wasn't doing you any good there in the ground. Take a rock and put it in the hole and pretend it is gold. That will serve the same purpose."

The moral of the story is this: Having something without enjoying it or using it for good is worthless. Each of us has been given many good gifts—not just money, but human gifts like the ability to sing, to dance, to draw, to help others, and so on. If we hide our gifts away without ever using them, then, like the gold in the can, they are of no use to us or to anyone else. But if we take our gifts out of hiding and use them, then everyone is blessed.

FOLLOW-UP: Work with the children to make a list of the varied gifts they have been given that they can share with the wider community.

2. Based on one of *Aesop's Fables.*

13

Turning a Problem into Something Good
Problems Can Become Opportunities for Service

SCRIPTURE: Mark 6:30–44 GNT

OBJECT FOR SHARING: A symbol of the American Red Cross

PRESENTATION: This lesson would be appropriate on a day when Holy Communion is being celebrated.

Have you ever seen one of these before? (*Hold up American Red Cross symbol for all to see*). Do you recognize this symbol? Perhaps you have seen this symbol on a flag, or on an emergency vehicle in your neighborhood, or at a blood drive. That's right, it is the symbol of the American Red Cross.

The American Red Cross was started because of a problem. Well, because of *many* problems, actually. Does anyone know who started the American Red Cross? It was Clara Barton. About 150 years ago during the Civil War, Clara Barton went to the battlefields to be a nurse, to care for soldiers who had been wounded. And then later she went to towns that had been flooded and helped those people who had lost everything in the floodwaters. For a while she went to Europe and helped start hospitals. She saw the good work that people were doing over there in Europe to help people who were suffering. And then she came back to America and said, "We need an organization whose sole purpose is to help people who are victims of disasters, like hurricanes, floods, fires, and such." And so Clara Barton started the American Red Cross.

Now whenever there is a flood, the American Red Cross volunteers will be there to pass out food and water and blankets and such. Whenever someone's home burns, the American Red Cross will be there to help the family find a new place to stay.

When someone is in an accident and loses a lot of blood and needs a transfusion, often it is the American Red Cross that has collected that blood and makes it available.

But the American Red Cross was started because of a problem. This goes to show that sometimes out of problems good things can grow.

So, whenever we have a problem in our lives, it is good if we can remember to pray to God: "Dear God, help me take this problem and turn it into something good."

FOLLOW-UP: Show and discuss a short video of the American Red Cross in action.

14
Five Kernels of Corn
A Legend About the Pilgrims Teaches Us to Be Thankful

SCRIPTURE: Ephesians 5:19–20 GNT

OBJECTS FOR SHARING: A few ears of "Indian corn" for show. Also, enough see-through snack bags containing five kernels each of "Indian corn" and the brief story printed below so each child can have one.

PRESENTATION: This story is perfect for the Sunday before or after Thanksgiving Day.

You may remember that it was the Pilgrims who came to America in 1620 who gave us the idea of a Thanksgiving Day celebration. Soon after the Pilgrims arrived in America, they discovered corn—Indian corn. The Native Americans taught the Pilgrims how to plant corn. The corn that the Native Americans shared with the Pilgrims and taught them to grow helped the Pilgrims to survive in those difficult early years.

But one year the harvest was not very good. Then some unexpected guests from England arrived and needed to be fed, which the Pilgrims did. But their food supplies started to run low. As winter came and their food supplies got smaller and smaller, the Pilgrims started rationing how much each person could eat each day. Can anyone tell us what rationing is? Rationing is giving each person only so much food and saying, "Okay, this is all the food you get to eat all day today." This difficult period was called the "starving time." It is said that at one time they only had enough food for each person to have a mere five kernels of corn a day—nothing more.

Well, eventually spring came, and they could grow more food. But it is said that after that, whenever another day of thanksgiving came around, the Pilgrims would put five kernels of corn on each of their plates to remind them of their blessings and reasons for giving thanks:

> The first kernel reminded them of autumn beauty.
> The second kernel reminded them of their love for each other.
> The third kernel reminded them of God's love and care.
> The fourth kernel reminded them of their friends, especially their Native American brothers and sisters.
> The fifth kernel reminded them of their freedom.

And so, these five kernels of corn reminded the Pilgrims of five good reasons to give thanks. And they can do the same for us. They can remind us to give thanks for autumn beauty, our love for each other, God's love and care, our friends, and our freedom to worship. So I have a bag of five kernels of corn for each of you that you can take home and use this week to help you give thanks.

FOLLOW-UP: You may copy the following abbreviated story and include it in a bag of five kernels of corn for each child.

Five Kernels of Corn

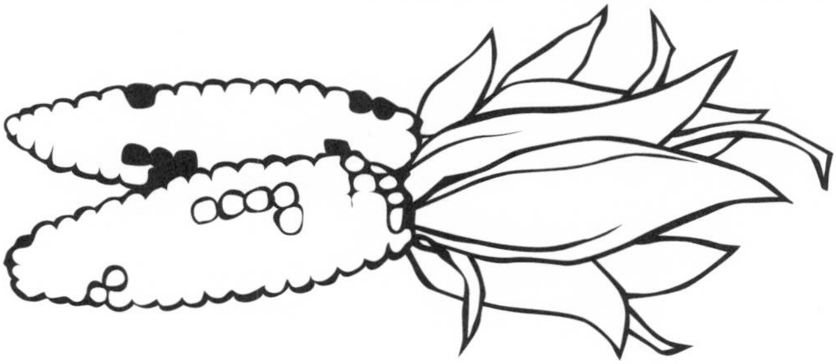

Soon after the Pilgrims arrived in America, they discovered corn—Indian corn. The Native Americans taught the Pilgrims how to plant corn. But one year the harvest was not very good. Their food supplies started to run low. It is said that at one time they only had enough food for each person to have a mere five kernels of corn a day—nothing more.

Well, eventually spring came, and they could grow more food. But it is said that after that, whenever another day of thanksgiving came around, the Pilgrims would put five kernels of corn on each of their plates to remind them of their blessings and reasons for giving thanks:

- The first kernel reminded them of autumn beauty.
- The second kernel reminded them of their love for each other.
- The third kernel reminded them of God's love and care.
- The fourth kernel reminded them of their friends, especially their Native American brothers and sisters.
- The fifth kernel reminded them of their freedom.

And so, these five kernels of corn reminded the Pilgrims of five good reasons to give thanks. And they can do the same for us.

15

Some Unusual Children's Toys

We Can Think of Ways to Provide Toys for Underprivileged Children

Scripture: Luke 3:7a, 10–11GNT

Objects for Sharing: A broken tree branch or stick eighteen inches or so long, a smooth stone, and a soda can.

Presentation: This lesson will work well between Thanksgiving and Christmas, when most people are thinking about sharing with others.

You never know what I am going to bring in my mystery bag, do you? Well, today I have brought some toys—some unique toys that many children around the world play with every day. What toys do you guess are in my bag? (*A doll, stuffed animal, ball, and the like may be suggested.*) Well, those are all good guesses, but incorrect.

Now, don't laugh, when I show you, but here is what I brought. First a stick (*remove a broken tree branch*). The only thing many children have to play with is a stick they pick up in the village or alongside the road. But they might also have a nice, smooth rock (*remove a smooth stone from the bag*). Perhaps they would use the stick to push the ball along on the ground, much like you and I would play miniature golf. Yet a third toy that many children might play with is a can (*drop a can on the floor and begin kicking it with your foot*). They might play kick the can sort of like you and I might play soccer.

The sad truth is, for many children around the world a stick, a rock, or a can may be all they have to play with. Either their parents don't have any money to buy toys, or there are no toys in their village or their country to be bought.

So I thought that during the next few weeks we might put our heads together with our parents and Sunday school teachers and see if we can't come up with a plan to collect some money to buy toys for children who have none. What do you think? Can we do that? I've brought along the first couple of dollars to get us started.

FOLLOW-UP: Lead the children in participating in a special collection for children in a developing country that may be directed through your denomination or other parachurch organization such as Church World Service.

16
Celebration of a King
As Children of God, All of Us Are Princesses and Princes

SCRIPTURE: 1 Timothy 6:15–16 GNT

OBJECT FOR SHARING: A king's crown, perhaps one used in Christmas pageants.

PRESENTATION: Consider this lesson for Reign of Christ or Christ the King Sunday, which is the last Sunday before the beginning of Advent.

A long, long time ago, in a land far, far away, a baby boy was born. The baby's parents were somewhat poor, so he grew up in a humble home where he watched his father work hard as he played on the floor beside him. Most people did not know it, but this baby boy was supposed to become a great king. But he grew up just like any other boy in his village, and no one really thought of him as being anything special.

Years went by. The boy grew and learned and one day became a teacher. He tried to teach people how to live their lives for God, as

though God were King and everything that is done in life should b
done to please this King.

But many people didn't want to hear what the teacher had to say
Living for God as the teacher taught was just too difficult. It require
too much of a sacrifice, and too much love for others.

So, they killed the teacher. Because they thought if they could kil
him, they could kill his message. But it didn't work. After he died, Go
caused him to live again. And the message he taught about love an
sacrifice spread all over the world.

And so before long people began to realize who this teacher reall
was. He *was* a King, God's *appointed* King, *the Ruler of the whole world*
And today we celebrate his kingship. It is the reign of King Jesus Chris
who shows us how to love and care for one another, and how to liv
together in peace.

And if Jesus is King, and if Jesus is God's Son, and if we are God
children too, then that would make us princes and princesses. And sc
you are Princess (*add child's name*) . . . And you are Prince (*add child
name*). . . .

FOLLOW-UP: Lead the children in making construction paper crown
with their prince or princess name written on them.

17

What Do You See?
Sometimes It Is Hard for Us to See Jesus

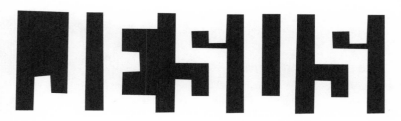

SCRIPTURE: Matthew 25:31–40 GNT

OBJECT FOR SHARING: One of the J E S U S eye-teaser plaques that can be purchased from Christian book and gift shops.

PRESENTATION: Maybe you will want to use this story during Advent when focus is on helping the poor.

I have brought something that someone gave to me. As I hold it up, I would like for you to look at it for a minute and then, when I ask you, tell me what you see. (*Hold up the J E S U S plaque for all to see.*) Don't say anything just yet. Give time for everyone to look at it and think about what they see.

Okay, what do you see? Well, when you first look at it, it just looks like dark pieces of wood glued on a board. Right? But then if you focus your eyes on the light spaces, it is easy to see the word JESUS. We might call this a brainteaser, or an eye teaser.

But, you know what? People have always had a hard time seeing Jesus for who he really was. There probably have been more books written about Jesus than anyone else in the history of the world. Even after two thousand years, people are still looking at Jesus and trying to see him for who he really was and is.

In the gospels, Jesus tells us that sometimes when we look at other people—the poor, the hungry, the thirsty, the sick, or the ones in prison—we are actually looking at him without knowing it. Sometimes Jesus longs to speak to us through another person, but we may not recognize him. We may not see Jesus when he passes our way.

There is a story in the gospel of Mark about a man who could not see physically with his eyes (*point to your eyes*), but he was able to recognize Jesus with his heart (*point toward your heart*) for who he really was.

That's what I hope for each of us—that we will be able to see Jesus for who he really is.

FOLLOW-UP: Perhaps you can secure someone who has a woodshop to help cut out enough pieces for every child to glue together a J E S U S plaque.

18

The Little Pebble
No One Noticed
Everyone, No Matter How "Small," Is Important

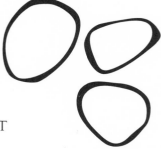

SCRIPTURE: Proverbs 30:24–28 GNT

OBJECT FOR SHARING: Small polished stones that can be purchased at craft supply stores.

PRESENTATION: This lesson could be used on a Sunday when you are celebrating children or baptizing an infant.

Have you ever been to visit a dam? Who can tell us what a dam is? One of the largest dams in the world is Hoover Dam, in the state of Nevada.

Today I have a story about a dam. But it's not about the whole dam, but rather about one tiny stone in the very big dam.

Once upon a time, there was a river that ran through a town. Many years ago, the leaders of the town built a stone dam across the river to help control the water when it rained a lot. And they were right. When the first week-long rainstorm came and the river started rising higher and higher, the dam helped control the water so it didn't run out of its banks and flood the people's homes.

Now, the dam was made of concrete and stones. Hundreds and thousands of stones. There was this one small stone that stuck out from the stone wall a little more than all the rest. But for years no one had ever noticed it. It was as though the little stone's entire existence was useless.

Many years passed. Then one day, some teenagers were playing around the base of the dam. One of the teenagers happened to look up and spy the one little stone that stuck out of the wall a little more than the rest. "There seems to be a little bit of water leaking from around that little stone," the teenager said to himself. Out of curiosity, he pulled on the stone a little, then went on his way.

Well, a few days went by. The massive body of water behind the dam kept pushing and pushing on that one little stone. The amount of water that was leaking from around the stone got greater and greater. The water pushed, and the little stone moved. And finally, SWOOSH! The water finally popped the little stone out of the wall, and it went sailing through the air and plopped down into the river.

Well, this could have spelled disaster. Luckily, city officials soon happened by and saw the stream of water—that looked like someone had planted a garden hose in the middle of the dam—shooting out from the dam. They were able to send divers down inside the dam to plug the hole from the inside. Then they sent stonemasons to the outside and with concrete and another small stone repaired the leak. Happily, the town was saved.

So, whenever you start feeling down on yourself, when you feel you're small and insignificant, remember the story of the one small stone that nobody ever noticed—until it wasn't there.

And I have a small stone for each of you to take with you as a reminder of how important you are and how much you would be missed if you were not here.

FOLLOW-UP: Share photos (perhaps online) of different dams and discuss how important dams are to us by generating energy, assisting in irrigation, flood control, and so on.

19

Under God's Wings

God Longs to Care For Us Like a Mother Hen Does Her Chicks

SCRIPTURE: Matthew 23:37 GNT

OBJECT FOR SHARING: A copy of Greg K. Olsen's picture of Jesus lamenting over Jerusalem, titled "O Jerusalem."

PRESENTATION: If possible, have a copy of Olsen's picture of Jesus lamenting over Jerusalem to share.

Have any of you ever visited a farm or a petting zoo and seen a mother hen with her baby chicks?

Well, if a mother hen senses danger, she raises her wings and runs and gathers her baby chicks under her wings and whisks them off to safety.

One day, as Jesus stood looking down at the city of Jerusalem, he became very sad. And he thought about the image of the mother hen gathering her baby chicks under her wings. And Jesus said, "O Jerusalem, Jerusalem; how I long to gather your children together as a mother hen protects her chicks beneath her wings." Someone has painted a picture of the scene, of Jesus sadly looking down at the city of Jerusalem. You see, Jesus knew that trouble would come to the people of Jerusalem, and he wished he could protect them like a mother hen protects her chicks.

That's the picture that Jesus also gives us of God. God is like the loving mother hen who wants to gather her babies under her wings to protect them. But, you know what? In order for God to do that, we have to be willing to let God care for us. As Jesus well knew, for God to be able to care for us like God wants to, we must be willing to follow where God leads us.

FOLLOW-UP: To view Olsen's picture "O Jerusalem," of Jesus lamenting over Jerusalem, go to http://www.artusa.com/olsen_prints3.htm and scroll down. You might also share other pictures of animals protecting their young.

20
A Ring for You
The Ring Can Be a Sign of Belonging

SCRIPTURE: Luke 15:11–24 GNT

OBJECT FOR SHARING: Any variety of "valuable" rings that might help illustrate the story.

PRESENTATION: If possible, secure enough toy rings from a dollar store so you can give one to each child. But make sure they are safe and free of lead.

Good morning! Is anyone wearing a ring today? I am wearing a couple of rings. One is a wedding ring that says I am special to someone else. And the other is my seminary (*or high school or college*) class ring that shows when I graduated.

When I was your age, I always wanted a ring for my finger. Why is it that people want to wear rings, do you suppose? Rings tell others something about us, as in the case of a high school, college, or seminary ring. Rings make us feel special, especially if that ring happens to be a big, shiny diamond ring. And rings give us a sense of belonging, as in the case when we "belong" to a husband, wife, or partner.

Well, in the Gospel of Luke, Jesus talks about a ring. Does anyone remember the story? That is right. When the long lost prodigal son returns home, the father gives him a ring to make him feel special, and to make him feel that he belongs to the family again. You see, the ring could have been a family ring, with the family's name or symbol on it. Sometimes such rings were used to seal important documents. They were called signet rings. When an important document was signed, then it would be folded and sealed with a drop of hot wax, and then the person signing it would press the family ring in the hot wax as an official seal.

Jesus is saying that God is like the loving father who gives a special ring to the son who comes home. God would like to give every one of us here this morning a special ring as a way of saying, "You are special to me. You are important. You are a member of my family."

Well, as God's representative, I would like to give each of you a ring as a sign of God's love and as a reminder that you are a special child of God.

_____

FOLLOW-UP: Lead the children in writing a letter to their families and then sealing them (very carefully and cautiously!) with letter wax, candle wax, a dab of molding clay, or melted crayon with a ring bearing a symbol.

21
The Shepherd's Crook
The Good Shepherd Guides Us through Life

SCRIPTURE: Psalm 23 GNT

OBJECT FOR SHARING: A model shepherd's crook

PRESENTATION: Plan this lesson for a Sunday when Psalm 23 is one of the readings of the day.

Good morning! Can anyone guess what this is? It is a shepherd's crook, or shepherd's staff. It is one of the two primary tools of the shepherd, the other being a rod or club. What do you suppose a shepherd would use a rod or club for? That's right—to protect his sheep by fighting off wild beasts.

And what do you suppose a shepherd would use a crook or staff for? A crook or staff is used to guide and care for the sheep. Suppose a sheep wandered off and got stuck in a briar patch. The shepherd could take the crook end of the staff and reach into the briar patch and pull the sheep out.

The staff is also used to guide the sheep along the trail, to keep them from straying. As the shepherd walks with the sheep, he can reach out the staff and use it to guide the sheep away from danger. The staff is a wonderful tool for the shepherd to guide the sheep.

The Bible says, "The Lord is my shepherd; your rod and your staff, they comfort me." If the real-life shepherd uses a staff to guide the sheep, what do you suppose is God's staff that helps to guide us? I am inclined to think that the "staff" that God uses to guide us is our conscience, that little voice in our head that tells us what is right.

You know when you are tempted to do something, and a little voice in your head says, "Liam, that is not the right thing to do." Or "Katherine, you shouldn't go there." That voice, I think, can be the way that God is trying to guide us to keep us safe and happy.

So when we hear that little voice that is telling us the right thing to do, try to remember the shepherd's staff. And just as the shepherd uses the staff to guide the sheep in right paths, so God is trying to guide us in the right paths too.

FOLLOW-UP: Lead the children in making paper maché shepherd's staffs.

22
A New Way of Making Friends
Kindness to Our Enemies Can Sometimes Result in Them Becoming Our Friends

SCRIPTURE: Acts 16:16–34 GNT

OBJECT FOR SHARING: Photograph of someone in prison

PRESENTATION: This story would fit well near the Martin Luther King Jr. holiday.

What would you think if you were walking down the street, doing nothing wrong, when the city police arrested you, beat you, and then threw you into jail? How would that make you feel? Would you be happy? Would you be nice to those who arrested you?

There is a story in the Bible that tells how Paul and his friends were walking down the street telling people about Jesus when the city guards arrested them, had them beaten, and threw them in a dirty, stinking prison. Now, you would think that Paul and his friends would be angry, and banging their tin cup on the prison bars demanding to be released. But not so. Instead, they started singing. And they sang throughout the night.

Then a miracle happened. An earthquake shook the prison so that the doors flew open. Paul and his friends could have escaped. But they didn't. Instead they just sat there. Well, the jailer ran in thinking that they would be gone and he would be in trouble for letting them escape.

Paul and his friends were so nice and kind to the jailer that he wanted to learn about Jesus and be baptized. So Paul taught him and his family. And, in turn, the jailer and his family doctored their wounds and fed them a nice meal.

Because of the kindness of Paul and his friends toward their enemies, those enemies became great friends and followers of Jesus.

It is hard to be kind to our enemies. But if we can find a way to do that, then sometimes our enemies can become our friends. And they might even become friends of Jesus too.

FOLLOW-UP: Share with the children names of some famous people who were arrested and imprisoned for doing what was right (George Fox, Dietrich Bonhoeffer, Martin Luther King Jr., and so on) or who became friends with their erstwhile enemies.

23
Wonderfully Made
God Is the Divine Potter Who Makes Us Wonderful and Beautiful

SCRIPTURES: Genesis 2:7; Psalm 139:14 NRSV

OBJECT FOR SHARING: Pottery

PRESENTATION: If possible, ask a potter to bring clay and a potter's wheel and work on it throughout the worship service.

Do you know what is one of the oldest forms of art in the world? That's right—pottery making. Archaeologists—persons who dig in the earth to uncover things people of long ago left behind—often find broken pieces of pottery that are thousands of years old. Why do you think pottery is one of the oldest forms of art known to humankind? Perhaps it is because pottery is such a necessity. People need jars and bowls and pots to store food in, cook in, and eat and drink from.

But you know what is one of the oldest forms of pottery in the world? Humans—men and women and boys and girls. One of the two creation stories in the Bible describes God shaping human beings from the clay of the earth, like a potter does.

So today we can think of God as the Master Potter who creates each one of us different. I am "wonderfully" (NRSV) or "marvelously" (*The Message*) made, the psalmist sings. Turn to the person next to you and say, "You are wonderfully made!" (*The adults can do that too, if you like—turn to the person next to you and say, "You are wonderfully made."*)

Just as a potter continues to work with the clay, so God wants to work with us each day——to make us more and more beautiful on the inside just as we have been made wonderful on the outside.

FOLLOW-UP: Have enough modeling clay for all the children to work with following the story time.

24
Little and Lost
God Cares for Every Little Thing

Scripture: Luke 15:8–10 GNT

Object for Sharing: A quart zipper-lock bag of ninety-nine pennies. Prior to the gathering, hide one penny somewhere in the worship space under the pews or chairs.

Presentation: This story will work well on a Sunday when the focus is on missions.

Good morning! Do you see what I have with me this morning? That's right, a bag of pennies. Would anyone like to guess how many pennies I have? Well, there were supposed to be one hundred pennies in my bag. But earlier this morning I let one of the pennies roll down the floor under the pews. Now, do you think I was going to get down on my hands and knees, in my good clothes, and look for that one penny? No, I wasn't. It was too much trouble, I thought to myself, for just one penny. In fact, as much as I like finding money on the sidewalk, I usually won't bend over to pick up a penny. A quarter sure, but usually not a penny.

However, in today's gospel reading from Luke, Jesus teaches us that God is not like that. There is a difference between us and God. Jesus says that God would go looking for the smallest coin. Well, it's not that God actually goes looking for coins, is it? What Jesus was trying to say with this picture is that just as someone might go looking for the smallest coin in the world, God is a God who goes looking for every single person in the world, no matter how small they might be. God loves every one of us and every one you know and every one you pass on the street. And when anyone feels lost from God's love, God searches for that person until that person is found and feels loved by God again.

FOLLOW-UP: Arrange with the treasurer beforehand to let the children count and roll coins to be given to some mission project that ministers to "the lost."

25
Putting Out the Fire
We Overcome Hatred
With Love for Our Enemies

SCRIPTURE: Romans 12:20–21 GNT

OBJECTS FOR SHARING: A picture of fire and a fire extinguisher.

PRESENTATION: Beforehand, prepare a clear cover sheet bearing the word "Hatred" that can be transposed over the picture of fire.

I am going to ask you to use your imaginations this morning. As you look at this picture, what do you see? That's right—fire. Fire is very dangerous, isn't it? That is why it is so important never to play with matches, or lighters, or candles. It only takes a short time for a tiny match or candle flame to become a raging fire that can destroy a home or even dozens of homes.

But my question this morning is this: Once a fire is started, what should be used to put it out? How about dousing it with cooking oil?

NO! How about gasoline? NO! How about throwing more fire onto it? NO! We've all heard the saying, "You can't fight fire with fire."

Actually, what is used to fight a fire depends on what kind of fire it is. If it is a grease, oil, or gasoline fire, it might be appropriate to fight it with some kind of powder, such as is in a fire extinguisher. If it is a leaf or grass fire, then we could fight it with water. You get the idea. But you can't fight fire with fire, as they say.

Now, imagine with me that this fire is the fire of HATRED. We hear about the fire of hatred on the news every day. Gang fights at high schools. Hatred and fighting between people of different races and different religions. How can we respond to the fire of hatred? With more hatred? No. More hatred only makes matters worse, leading to more hatred and fighting.

People like Jesus, Gandhi, and Martin Luther King Jr. have taught us that the best way to fight the fire of hatred is with love, and by being kind to our enemies, and by praying for our enemies.

You see, often we don't know what it is in their lives that makes some people so unhappy that they think they have to respond with hate. So as you go out into the world and see the fire of hatred, as much as you can, try to put it out with love and kindness and by praying for those who build the fires of hate.

FOLLOW-UP: Invite the children to share instances when others did things to hurt them, how they responded, and ways they might have responded that would have led to a peaceful solution.

26
What Happened to That Gold?
What We Give Goes to Meet Real Needs

SCRIPTURE: Matthew 2:1–12 GNT

OBJECT FOR SHARING: A small chest full of gold coins

PRESENTATION: This lesson will work best on Epiphany Sunday.

Do you remember the three gifts that the wise men, or magi, presented to the baby Jesus? Correct—gold, incense (frankincense), and myrrh. Today, let's just think about the gold. What do you suppose happened to the gold that the wise men gave to the baby Jesus? Have you ever thought about it? Do you suppose that Mary and Joseph locked it away in a treasure chest to send Jesus to college some day? Do you suppose they had it carved into crown? Do you suppose they had it melted down to make gold eating utensils? Or do you suppose they had the gold carved into a pretty statue? I am guessing that they did none of those things.

Probably Mary and Joseph used the gift of gold to meet their family's real needs. Maybe they used it to buy food or to pay for lodging as they traveled from one place to the next. Or maybe they used it to buy clothing for the baby Jesus, or ointment to put on his diaper rash. I am guessing that Mary and Joseph used the wise men's gold to meet the real, day-to-day needs that little Jesus had as he grew up.

You see, Jesus doesn't really need crowns of gold, or pretty statues, or anything like that. When we give our gold—our offerings—Jesus wants them to go to meeting real needs of real people: supplying food for the hungry, helping provide a warm place to sleep for those on the streets, and so on. And Jesus said that whenever we give to someone in need in his name, it is like we are giving to Jesus himself.

Real gold, real money, for real needs. I think that is what the wise men's gold was used for. And we, too, can meet real needs when we give our offerings in Jesus' name.

FOLLOW-UP: Brainstorm with the children about some real needs in your local community that your church might help meet through its offerings.

Annotated Resources

Anderson, Herbert, and Foley, Edward. *Mighty Stories, Dangerous Rituals: Weaving Together the Human and the Divine.* San Francisco: Jossey-Bass, 1998.
> Discusses the power of religious ritual and myth and how they help us create and express meaning. Shows how ritual and myth connect the human and divine.

Bettelheim, Bruno. *The Uses of Enchantment: The Meaning and Importance of Fairy Tales.* New York: Alfred A. Knopf, 1976.
> An invaluable resource in the theory of how children's tales should arouse curiosity, stimulate the imagination, help children discover their self-identity and deal with inner conflicts, and confront their fears and problems.

Cameron, Julia. *The Artist's Way.* New York: G.P. Putnam's Sons, 1992.
> Cameron seeks, through practical guidance, to bring out the creative energy, what she refers to as "God energy," that is within all of us.

Campbell, Joseph. With Bill Moyers. *The Power of Myth.* New York: Doubleday, 1988.
> This work highlights exactly what the title suggests: the power of religious myths. Much is said about the hero that "lurks in each one of us."

Coles, Robert. *The Spiritual Life of Children.* Boston: Houghton Mifflin Company, 1990.
> A wealth of wisdom has been gleaned and shared from Coles' interviews with hundreds of children from a number of religious backgrounds. This work reveals the great depth of thought in religious matters that children are capable of when given a chance to express themselves.

Estes, Clarissa Pinkola, ed. *Tales of the Brothers Grimm.* New York: Quality Paperback Book Club, 1999.
> In her introduction to the *Tales of the Brothers Grimm*, Estes discusses soul life, innate ideals, and universal thoughts. A good resource for those interested in universal thoughts and archetypes.

Fahs, Sophia L. *Jesus the Carpenter's Son.* Boston: Beacon Press, 1945.
> Fahs uses the imagination (and indirectly encourages the modern presenter of children's sermons) to fill in the blanks and address the "What ifs" that surround the life of Jesus.

Fahs, Sophia. L. *Today's Children and Yesterday's Heritage*. Boston: Beacon, 1952.
In this work Fahs stresses the importance of a child's self-worth, the child's sense of relationship with the larger world, the need to "feel the Mystery of Life," and the interdependence of all life.

Groome, Thomas H. *Christian Religious Education*. San Francisco: Harper Collins, 1980.
Groome speaks of the importance of lived faith, becoming what we are called to become, and nurturing human freedom and creativity.

Hammer, Randy. *Everyone a Butterfly: 40 Sermons for Children*. Boston: Skinner House Books, 2004.
In addition to forty children's sermons that follow the church year beginning in September and ending in June, this collection includes an introduction that discusses the theory of sermon preparation for children and what makes for a "successful" children's sermon. Each entry includes a suggested object for sharing, suggestions for presentation, and possible follow-up activities.

Hammer, Randy. *The Talking Stick: 40 Children's Sermons with Activities*. Cleveland: Pilgrim Press, 2007.
Following the same format as the present volume, the forty stories and lessons in *The Talking Stick* generally follow the church calendar. A number of them aquaint listeners with historic figures, such as Brother Lawrence, Martin Luther, and Phyllis Wheatley. The stories encourage respect for everyone created in the Divine image, and seek to instill such positive qualities as service, hospitality, unity, stewardship of the earth, truthfulness, peacemaking, and the like.

Handford, S. A., translator. *Aesop's Fables*. New York: Penguin, 1994.
Brief moral tales, many of which can easily be adapted for use with children in worship. In the introduction, Handford discusses the "common-sense and folk wisdom" at the heart of stories and fables.

Harris, Maria. *Fashion Me a People*. Louisville: Westminster John Knox Press, 1989.
Harris notes the importance of spending time alone "in the company of the Divine."

Jordan, Jerry Marshall. *Filling Up the Brown Bag* (a children's sermon how-to book). New York: Pilgrim Press, 1987.
An invaluable resource, Jordan stresses the importance of letting children know they are loved and wanted, nurturing within them an awareness of God, instilling within them a sense of self-worth and a positive self-image, encouraging them to stretch themselves and reach their full potential, and sparking their imaginations by getting them to say "I see!"

Lipman, Doug. *Improving Your Storytelling: Beyond the Basics for All Who Tell Stories in Work or Play.* Atlanta: August House, 1999.
    A work that goes beyond the basics for storytellers, this work is a good resource for those who seek to perfect the storytelling craft.

MacDonald, Margaret Read. *The Story-Teller's Start-Up Book: Finding, Learning, Performing and Using Folktales.* Little Rock, Ark.: August House, 1993.
    A very helpful work that gives practical guidance on finding, preparing, and telling folktales and other stories.

Rogers, Fred. *Play Time.* Philadelphia: Running Press, 2001.
    A good resource, most notably for preschoolers, for planning follow-up activities utilizing common household objects. Encourages children's use of imagination and creativity.

Rogers, Fred. *You Are Special.* Philadelphia: Running Press, 2002.
    A tiny pocket book of timeless wisdom that reinforces the truth that everyone is special and that can easily be worked into many children's sermons.

Sawyer, Ruth. *The Way of the Storyteller.* New York: Penguin, 1970.
    This work is a well-known classic on the art of storytelling that should be read by everyone who has a real interest in storytelling.

Silf, Margaret, ed. *100 Wisdom Stories from Around the World.* Cleveland: Pilgrim Press, 2003.
    Though written primarily from an adult viewpoint, many of these wonderful stories can be adapted for use with children.

Wagner, Betty Jane. *Dorothy Heathcote: Drama as a Learning Medium.* Revised ed. Portland, Me.: Calendar Islands Publishers, 1999.
    Though written as a resource for leading children in drama, this is also a good resource—especially the first half—on how to physically lead children's sermons. Discusses the discovery of human experience, reaching a deeper insight, helping children catch a vision of the wider world, and the importance of tapping the energy of the human spirit and valuing human achievement.

White, William R. *Stories for Telling: A Treasury for Christian Storytellers.* Minneapolis: Augsburg, 1986.
    In addition to providing some good introductory material on storytelling in ministry, this work shares a great number of stories, folktales and fables from a variety of sources that can be used or adapted for children's sermons.

Supply List

Chapter 1: The Singing Bowl
- Bronze singing bowl and baton

Chapter 2: A Hard Shell or a Soft Shell?
- Coconut
- Sponge Nerf ball

Chapter 3: Who Is This Man?
- Picture of a small boat on the Sea of Galilee
- Fishing gear

Chapter 4: Through the Dark Forest
- Picture of a dark forest
- Picture of Dorothy in *The Wizard of Oz*
- Video clip from *The Wizard of Oz* in the dark forest

Chapter 5: Salt Locked in a Box
- Small, lockable treasure chest
- Salt
- Small lock

Chapter 6: Birds Don't Have Hands
- Picture of your favorite bird

Chapter 7: Spilled Milk Can't Be Gathered Back Up
- Bowl of dry sand
- Glass of milk

Chapter 8: Good Morning! And Welcome to Wal-Mart!
- Smiley face stickers, yellow if possible

Chapter 9: Something Beautiful for God
- Rough piece of wood
- Carving tool
- Handicraft made from wood
- Short video clip of craftsperson in action

Chapter 10: Giving What We Have
- Bottle of perfume
- Sweet-smelling spices
- Aromatic flowers
- Olive oil

Chapter 11: Good for Nothing
- Bill for services rendered

Chapter 12: Coffee Can Faith
- Coffee can full of coins

Chapter 13: Turning a Problem into Something Good
- Symbol of the American Red Cross
- Short video of American Red Cross volunteers in action

Chapter 14: Five Kernels of Corn
- Several ears of "Indian corn"
- Small plastic zipper bags

Chapter 15: Some Unusual Children's Toys
- Twig or stick about eighteen inches long
- Smooth stone

🖐 Soda can
🖐 A dollar bill or two

Chapter 16: Celebration of a King
🖐 King's crown, the type used in a Christmas pageant
🖐 Construction paper
🖐 Markers

Chapter 17: What Do You See?
🖐 J E S U S eye-teaser plaque
🖐 Wood pieces to make J E S U S plaques

Chapter 18: The Little Pebble No One Noticed
🖐 Small, polished stones
🖐 Photos of famous dams

Chapter 19: Under God's Wings
🖐 Copy of Greg K. Olsen's picture of Jesus lamenting over Jerusalem, titled "O Jerusalem."
🖐 Pictures of animals protecting their young

Chapter 20: A Ring for You
🖐 Variety of rings (class ring, wedding ring, etc.)
🖐 Inexpensive toy ring for every child
🖐 Letter wax, candle wax, molding clay, or melted crayons
🖐 Ring with which to make impression in the wax

Chapter 21: The Shepherd's Crook
🖐 Shepherd's crook
🖐 Supplies to make paper maché staffs

Chapter 22: A New Way of Making Friends
🖐 Picture of someone sitting in prison

Chapter 23: Wonderfully Made

- 🖐 Pieces of pottery
- 🖐 Potter's wheel
- 🖐 Modeling clay

Chapter 24: Little and Lost

- 🖐 Small see-through zipper-lock bag
- 🖐 One hundred pennies
- 🖐 Coins and paper coin sleeves for rolling

Chapter 25: Putting Out the Fire

- 🖐 Picture of fire
- 🖐 Fire extinguisher

Chapter 26: What Happened to That Gold?

- 🖐 Small treasure chest
- 🖐 Gold coins

About the Author

Randy Hammer

Randy Hammer has over thirty years of experience in pastoral ministry. He has worked with children in Vacation Church School, outdoor ministry, and of course, during the children's sermon time. His number one passion in ministry has been the preparation and delivery of sermons. Other passions include writing poetry and devotional materials, woodworking, and spending time with his wife, children, and their grandchildren.

He is the author of *Dancing in the Dark: Lessons in Facing Life's Challenges with Courage and Creativity* (1999, The Pilgrim Press), *Everyone a Butterfly: Forty Sermons for Children* (2004, Skinner House), *The Talking Stick: 40 Children's Sermons with Activities* (2007, The Pilgrim Press), and *52 Ways to Ignite Your Congregation… Practical Hospitality* (2009, The Pilgrim Press).

Phyllis Vos Wezeman, Anna L. Liechty,
and Kenneth R. Wezeman

ISBN 0-8298-1519-8
paper/96 pages/$10.00

TOUCH THE WATER
30 Children's Sermons on Baptism

Phyllis Vos Wezeman, Anna L. Liechty,
and Kenneth R. Wezeman

ISBN 0-8298-1518-X
112 pages/paper/$10.00

PLANTINGS SEEDS OF FAITH

Virginia H. Loewen

ISBN 0-8298-1473-6
96 pages/paper/$10.00

GROWING SEEDS OF FAITH

Virginia H. Loewen

ISBN 0-8298-1488-4
96 pages/paper/$10.00

THE BROWN BAG

Jerry Marshall Jordan

ISBN 0-8298-0411-0
117 pages/paper/$9.95

SMALL WONDERS
Sermons for Children

Glen E. Rainsley

ISBN 0-8298-1252-0
104 pages/paper/$12.95

TIME WITH OUR CHILDREN
Stories for Use in Worship, Year B

Dianne E. Deming

ISBN 0-8298-0952-X
182 pages/paper/$9.95

TIME WITH OUR CHILDREN
Stories for Use in Worship, Year C

Dianne E. Deming

ISBN 0-8298-0953-8
157 pages/paper/$9.95

To order these or any other books from The Pilgrim Press call or write to:

The Pilgrim Press
700 Prospect Avenue East
Cleveland, Ohio 44115-1100

Phone orders: 1-800-537-3394 • Fax orders: 216-736-2206
Please include shipping charges of $6.00 for the first book and
$1.00 for each additional book.
Or order from our web sites at
www.pilgrimpress.com and www.ucpress.com.

Prices subject to change without notice.